LONGMAN AMERICAN BUSINESS E

SOCIAL SKILLS FOR BUSINESS PEOPLE

ALL WORK & NO PLAY

Longman

LINDSEY NICOLL
Series editors Andrew Vaughan and Neil Heyen

With thanks
to my parents

Pearson Education Limited,
Edinburgh Gate, Harlow,
Essex CM20 2JE, England
and Associated Companies throughout the world.

First published 1994
Fourth impression 1999

Printed in China
EPC/04

ISBN 0 582 08421 0

Acknowledgements

We are grateful to the following for their permission to reproduce copyright photographs:

J. Allan Cash Photo Library for page 54 (middle, bottom). The Image Bank/Steve Niedorf for page 22 (right), /Kaz Mori for page 35. Pictor International for pages 22 (left), 23 (right), 54 (top). Chris Ridgers for page 17. Tony Stone Worldwide for page 23 (left), 28, 29. Telegraph Colour Library for page 46. Zefa Picture Library (UK) Limited for pages 9, 25.

Designed by Giles Davies.

Illustrated by George Parkins and Jerry Collins.

Picture Research by Penni Bickle.

Cover Photograph by Longman Photographic Unit.

Special thanks to UCM, Hove, for their assistance in the production of this title.

Contents

About the Series

This text is one of a series of American English business textbooks designed for lower intermediate students. The titles in the series reflect some of the activities that students at this level are frequently asked to perform. The aim of the series is primarily to provide support for specific areas of business performance rather than to improve overall language proficiency. The texts are ideal supplements to longer, more general courses, and can also be used individually in a short course, or in combination with each other to form a longer course.

We strongly feel that the most valuable resource in any Business English course is the students themselves. The role of the instructor in such a course is to draw on, and provide the language support for, the real life experiences and needs of the students. Through all of the texts we try to put the focus on the students' work outside of the classroom. In our experience, the more a personal connection can be made between what goes on in the classroom and what happens on-the-job, the more successful a course will be.

About the Book

All Work and No Play is designed to teach socializing language skills to lower intermediate level students. It is best suited to classroom use, but can also be used for self-study purposes, as there is an answer key at the end of the book, as well as an accompanying cassette tape and transcripts.

While many lower level students can discuss technical or business matters with some degree of confidence, they often lack the ability to feel comfortable using English in social situations which involve people from different cultural backgrounds. This book helps students bridge that gap.

Because the book is designed for lower intermediate students, each unit includes clear presentation of useful language, listening activities, guided language activities followed by freer practice and, finally, a role-play situation which allows students to combine the main target language skills presented in the unit. Throughout all the units, however, there is a strong emphasis on *performance* by students themselves in a variety of socializing situations frequently experienced in the business world.

There is also an emphasis on degrees of formality and informality, since feedback has indicated that an awareness of this issue is important even at this lower level of proficiency.

The book should also encourage students to become more aware of possible cross-cultural differences which they may encounter when socializing with businesspeople from other countries.

The book can be used for intensive or extensive courses, and can also be used in conjunction with the other language texts in the series, or with such books as *Ready for Business* or *Functioning in Business,* also published by Longman.

Using the Book

All Work and No Play can be used as a continuous course, starting from *Unit 1* and ending with *Unit 6*. This would be a good way to use the book with particularly low-level students. Alternatively, it can be used as a resource to be dipped into. There is no storyline and each unit is free-standing. Using the book in this way will allow instructors to meet the particular needs and priorities of their students.

All six units follow a broadly similar format. Key language points are presented in the form of a listening text.

Pre-Listening Questions

These questions are designed to make the students think about the situation before listening to the tape. If the class level is particularly low, the instructor could introduce difficult vocabulary at this stage. Suggested time: 5-10 minutes.

Listening Activity 1: True—False

These true-false questions are designed to check the students' general understanding of the listening passage. The instructor should read through the items first to make sure that everyone understands them, before playing the tape. The students can be encouraged to compare answers with each other before whole-class correction of the section. If there are any disagreements, the instructor can play the tape again. Suggested time: 10-15 minutes.

Listening Activity 2: Dialogue completion

In this section, the focus is on the forms of the target language described in the Unit Focus.

This section contains the complete dialogue with certain key phrases missing. The instructor should let the students read through the passage before playing the tape. In order to allow the students time to write, the instructor should stop the tape at the end of sentences containing deleted portions. The students should be given at least two opportunities to listen to the tape before going over the answers. At the end of the first playing, students can compare their answers before the second playing. Suggested time: 20-30 minutes.

Presentation of Language, Notes and Related Activities

The listening section is followed by a number of sections in which key language functions from the dialogue are presented along with additional examples. These functions are then practiced through a variety of activities, beginning with more guided activities and culminating in freer activities where students are required to use their target language skills more independently.

Generally, the instructor should go over any sample language, as well as any additional explanations under the *Note* heading, and the students can then do the activities. The instructor should first model an item from the activity, perhaps using one of the stronger students.

Role-Play

This section is where the students "put it all together." They are given a situation in which they must perform the language functions practiced in the previous language sections.

It is a good idea to select a student (preferably one of the top students) and model the role-play once.

If a video camera is available, videotape and play back the role-plays. If the students are critiqued after role-playing, they should be allowed to repeat the role-play to give them the the chance to improve their performance.

It is important that students be encouraged to achieve effective communication as much as linguistic accuracy in these role-plays. Suggested time: 60-90 minutes. The time will vary depending on class size and type of role-play.

In general, the minimum time required for a unit will be anywhere from six to eight hours, making the book ideal for 60- to 80-hour courses. However, the book can also be used for longer courses.

UNIT

1 First Steps

UNIT FOCUS

- Introducing Yourself and Formal Greetings
- Small Talk
- Formal Leavetakings and Goodbyes

Have you ever visited a company overseas? Have you ever met an overseas visitor to your company? Where did you meet him or her? What language did you use? What did you talk about?

Activity 1

Mr. Ando is the new head of sales of Siba Pharmaceuticals in Tokyo. He is visiting the company's headquarters in San Francisco. Listen to the conversation and then mark the sentences true (T) or false (F).

1.	Ms. Tod has never met Mr. Ando.	T	F
2.	Ms. Tod is too busy to speak to Mr. Ando.	T	F
3.	The receptionist takes Mr. Ando into Ms. Tod's office.	T	F
4.	Ms. Tod offers Mr. Ando something to drink.	T	F
5.	Mr. Ando did not fly directly to San Francisco from Tokyo.	T	F
6.	Mr. Ando likes his hotel.	T	F

Activity 2

Listen to the conversation again and fill in the missing words or phrases.

MR. ANDO: [1]____________________ . [2]______________ Ken Ando. I'm the head of sales from the Tokyo office. I have an appointment with Ms. Tod.

RECEPTIONIST: Oh, yes, Mr. Ando. [3]____________________ . Ms. Tod is expecting you. Please go right in.

MR. ANDO: Thank you. [4]____________________ , Ms. Tod. [5]______________________________ Tokyo.

MS. TOD: Ah, yes, please come in, Mr. Ando.

MR. ANDO: [6]____________________ , Ms. Tod? It's [7]______________________________ you.

MS. TOD: [8]______________________________ ? [9]____________________ , too. Welcome to San Francisco. [10]____________________ your visit.

MR. ANDO: Thank you. [11]______________ I will.

MS. TOD: Please, take a seat. [12]__________________ some tea or coffee?

MR. ANDO: Thank you. I'd like coffee, please. Black with no sugar.

MS. TOD: Ms. Hind, could we have two coffees, please? One black with no sugar, and one with cream and no sugar. Well, Mr. Ando, 13 ________________________?

MR. ANDO: Yesterday morning.

MS. TOD: 14 ________________________?

MR. ANDO: 15 ________________ . I stopped off in Hawaii for a day to visit some friends, so I didn't have a long flight.

MS. TOD: That's good. And 16 ________________?

MR. ANDO: It's 17 ____________________ , and very 18 ____________.
It's right next to a bus stop.

MS. TOD: Ah, that's very important in San Francisco!

Introducing Yourself and Formal Greetings

Now look at these phrases from the conversation between Ms. Tod and Mr. Ando:

Good morning. My name is (Ken Ando).
How do you do, (Ms. Tod)?
It's nice to meet you.
How do you do, (Mr. Ando)?
It's nice to meet you, too.

Note:
The first time you meet someone, use a "formal" or "neutral" greeting like "How do you do?" rather than an "informal" greeting like "Hello" or "Hi."

Here are some more phrases you can use:

Speaker 1

Good { morning / afternoon. / evening. } I'm ________. / My name is _______. I'm from (company) in (town/country).

How do you do? { It's nice to meet you. / I'm pleased to meet you. / I'm delighted to meet you. }

Speaker 2

How do you do? { It's nice to meet you, too. / I'm pleased to meet you, too. / I'm delighted to meet you, too. }

Welcome to________. I hope you { enjoy your / have a pleasant } visit.

Speaker 1

Thank you. I'm sure I will.

Speaker 2

Did you have a good flight/journey?
How was your flight/journey?

Speaker 1

(Yes,) It was { fine, thank you. / not too bad, thank you. }

(No,) it { wasn't very good. / was awful. }

Speaker 2

Oh, I'm sorry to hear that.
Oh, that's too bad.

Activity 3 *Mr. Hyde is meeting Mr. Chu for the first time. Match the phrases on the left with the phrases on the right. Then place them in the correct order.*

1. Good afternoon. My name is Joe Hyde. I'm from Simax Computers in London.
2. How was your flight?
3. How do you do, Mr. Chu? I'm very pleased to meet you.

a. Oh, not too bad, thank you.
b. How do you do, Mr. Hyde? I'm Lee Chu.
c. Pleased to meet you too, Mr. Hyde.

Activity 4 *Work with a partner. You are meeting your partner for the first time at his/her company headquarters. Take turns as A and B.*

A	B
Introduce yourself.	Welcome your partner.
Greet your partner.	Ask him/her about the journey.
Tell him/her about your journey.	Wish him/her a pleasant visit.

Small Talk

Look at these questions from the conversation:

> When did you arrive?
> How was your flight?
> How is your hotel?

Note:
When you meet someone for the first time, it is usual to ask him/her some polite questions to show your interest. Be careful not to ask too personal questions—they may offend!

Did you have a good flight?

Activity 5

a. *What kind of questions can you ask when you meet a visitor for the first time? Discuss in pairs.*

b. *Look at the questions below.*
*Which are **suitable** and which are **unsuitable** questions to ask the first time you meet an American?*
Check the correct column.

Questions	Suitable	Unsuitable
1. Do you like living in (Japan)?		
2. What do you think of (capital city)?		
3. How much money do you earn a year?		
4. Do you play golf?		
5. What is your religion?		
6. Are you a member of a political party?		
7. Are you married?		
8. How old are you?		
9. What is the weather like in your country?		
10. What is the population of the USA?		
11. Do you have any children?		

Now decide which questions are suitable/unsuitable to ask someone from your country. Discuss your answers with the group.

Activity 6

Below is a list of general small talk topics to use when you meet someone for the first time.
In pairs, think of questions that you could ask about each topic. Write them in the spaces below each topic.

Example:
Topic: **Accommodation**
How is your hotel?
Where are you staying?

The Flight/Journey

Plans

The Visitor's Country

The Weather

Previous Visits to your Country

Accommodation

Now practice asking and answering the questions in pairs or small groups. Check the key for suggested questions.

Activity 7 *In the following conversation, write suitable responses in the spaces. Mr. Santos is from the Philippines.*

MS. THOMAS: Welcome to New York, Mr. Santos. I hope your flight was OK?

MR. SANTOS: 1 ______________________________.

MS. THOMAS: Is this your first visit to the United States?

MR. SANTOS: 2 ______________________________.

MS. THOMAS: Oh, where were you?

MR. SANTOS: 3 ______________________________.

MS. THOMAS: I see. Well, you'll find New York quite different!

4 ______________________________?

MR. SANTOS: I'm from San Fernando.

MS. THOMAS: 5 ______________________________?

MR. SANTOS: It's north of Manila.

MS. THOMAS: Ah, I see. 6 ______________________________?

MR. SANTOS: I'll probably be staying for four days. I have to go to Washington next week.

MS. THOMAS: Well, 7 ______________________________.

MR. SANTOS: Thank you, I'm sure I will!

Check the key for suggested responses.

Formal Leavetakings and Goodbyes

Activity 8 *Ms. Tod and Mr. Ando have finished their business discussion. Listen to the end of their conversation. Write what they say.*

MS. TOD: Well, 1 ______________________________.

I hope to see you again on Wednesday.

MR. ANDO: 2 ______________________________.

I'll see you on Wednesday. Thank you. 3 ____________.

MS. TOD: Goodbye.

Look at these phrases from the conversation:

It's been (very) nice meeting you.
It's been (very) nice meeting you, too.
I'll see you on Wednesday.
Goodbye.

Note:
If you know *when* you will see the other person, you can mention this before you say "Goodbye."
If you do not know when you will see the other person, you can say:

"I hope you enjoy your visit/trip/holiday."

Your Turn

Practice the following role-play with your partner.
Take turns as A and B.

A
You are the sales manager for a computer software company. You are visiting the head office of an advertising agency for the first time.

You meet B, the manager of the agency. Greet him or her and introduce yourself.

Answer B's questions.
You plan to stay in B's city for three days. You have been in the city once before. You find it very exciting. You will come back to the office in two days' time.

B
You are the manager of an advertising agency. You are meeting A for the first time in your head office. A is the sales manager of a computer software company.

Ask A where he or she is from, how long he or she plans to stay in your city, if it is his or her first visit and if he or she likes it.

UNIT
2 Moving On

UNIT FOCUS
- Informal Greetings
- Introducing Third Parties
- Informal Leavetakings and Goodbyes

Does your company send employees overseas? Where to? How long are the visits? What are the visits for?

Activity 1

Mr. Moon is visiting a paper mill near Toronto. Listen to the conversation and mark the sentences true (T) or false (F).

1	Mr. Bell and Mr. Moon already know each other.	T	F
2.	Mr. Hays and Mr. Moon have never met before.	T	F
3.	Mr. Moon and Mr. Bell are both single.	T	F
4.	Mr. Hays has visited Korea before.	T	F
5.	Mr. Moon knows Canada very well.	T	F
6.	Mr. Hays and Mr. Bell will never see each other again.	T	F

Activity 2

Listen to the conversation again and fill in the missing words or phrases.

MR. BELL: Oh, [1]________, Mr. Moon. It's [2]______________________________

______________________.

MR. MOON: [3]________, Mr. Bell. I'm pleased to see you again, too.

[4]__________________?

MR. BELL: I'm [5]_____________, thank you. And you?

MR. MOON: I'm fine. And [6]____________________________?

MR. BELL: They're all very well, thank you. What about your family?

[7]__________________?

MR. MOON: They're also very well.

MR. BELL: I'm glad to hear it. And you're still living in Pusan?

MR. MOON: Yes, but we moved to a bigger house last year.

MR. BELL: That's nice. Oh, there's my colleague, Mr. Hays. [8]_______,

Jim! Come and join us.

MR. HAYS: Hello, Pete! How [9]________________________?

MR. BELL: Fine, thanks. Let me [10]_____________ Mr. Moon.

He's from Korean Paper Corporation. Mr. Moon, [11]__________

____________ Mr. Hays? He's a [12]__________________________

in the Research and Development Department.

MR. MOON: [13]___________________, Mr. Hays? It's nice to meet you.

MR. HAYS: How do you do, Mr Moon? [14] ______________________.

Where [15] ______________________, Mr. Moon?

MR. MOON: I'm from Pusan. Do you know it?

MR. HAYS: No, but I visited Seoul two years ago. [16] ______________

______________ to Canada?

MR. MOON: Yes, it is.

MR. HAYS: What do you think of it?

MR. MOON: Well, it's quite different from Korea. There's so much space!

MR. HAYS: [17] ______________________________________?

MR. MOON: Well, my visit is for a week, but I may stay a few extra days.

MR. HAYS: I hope you enjoy your visit.

MR. MOON: Thank you. I'm sure I will.

MR. HAYS: [18] ______________, but I have to speak to my supervisor. It was nice meeting you, Mr. Moon.

MR. MOON: Nice meeting you, too. Goodbye.

MR. HAYS: [19] ______________________, Pete. [20] __________ .

MR. BELL: OK, [21] ______________________ . Bye.

Informal Greetings

Look at these phrases from the conversation:

Hello, (Mr. Moon)! It's nice to see you again!
Hello, (Mr. Bell)! I'm pleased to see you again, too.
How are you?
I'm very well, thank you. And you?
I'm fine.

Note:
Because Mr. Bell and Mr. Moon know each other already, they use the more neutral "Hello." After greeting someone you know, it is normal to ask how the other person is.

Here are some more examples for greeting someone you already know:

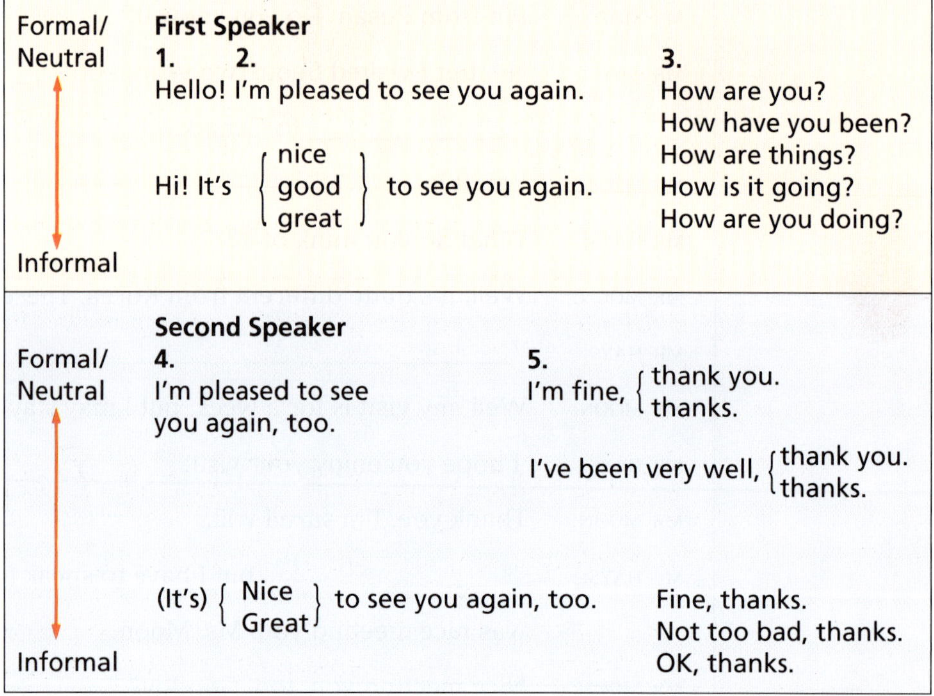

	First Speaker		
Formal/ Neutral	1.	2.	3.
	Hello!	I'm pleased to see you again.	How are you? How have you been? How are things? How is it going? How are you doing?
Informal	Hi!	It's { nice / good / great } to see you again.	

	Second Speaker	
Formal/ Neutral	4.	5.
	I'm pleased to see you again, too.	I'm fine, { thank you. / thanks. } I've been very well, { thank you. / thanks. }
Informal	(It's) { Nice / Great } to see you again, too.	Fine, thanks. Not too bad, thanks. OK, thanks.

Note:
When you meet someone you see often, or know very well, it is possible to leave out Steps 2 and 4 and go straight to Steps 3 and 5.

Activity 3 *Take turns practicing the phrases above with a partner.*

Activity 4 *Listen to the tape. Use the phrases above to help you respond to the speakers. (There are 5 examples.)*

Example:
You hear: Hello! It's great to see you again! How are you doing?
You answer: *Not too bad, thanks.*

Activity 5 *How would you greet the people in these situations? Write the phrases in the spaces.*

1. You are meeting an overseas business contact, Mr. Schmidt, for the first time at the airport.

____

____

2. You meet a business colleague at a trade fair. You have met him a few times before.

____

____

3. You have been away on a business trip for two weeks. You are now back in your office. You meet a colleague from your department.

____

____

With a partner, practice greeting and responding in the situations above.

Introducing Third Parties

Look at these phrases from the conversation:

> Let me introduce Mr. Moon. He's from Korean Paper Corporation.
> Mr. Moon, may I introduce Mr. Hays? He's a colleague of
> mine in the Research and Development department.

Note:
When we introduce other people, we say their names and usually give some other information—what company they are from, what they do, where they work, and so on.

Here are some more examples:

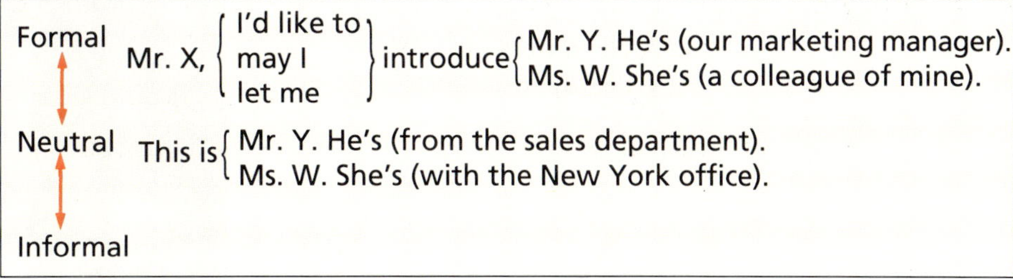

Activity 6 *Work in groups of three. Introduce each other. Move around the room.*

Example:

A: Mr. B, let me introduce Mr. C. He works in my office.
Mr. C, may I introduce Mr. B. He's from the accounts department.

B: How do you do, Mr. C? I'm pleased to meet you.

C: How do you do, Mr. B? I'm pleased to meet you, too.

Activity 7 *The people in the pictures are visiting your company. Introduce them to one of your colleagues.*
Work in groups of three. Take turns being the visitor. Ask the visitor follow-up questions.

Name: Mike Jones
From: The United States
Job: Computer programmer
Arrived here yesterday
Will stay four days

Name: Li Ha Bing
From: Hong Kong
Job: In domestic sales department in a branch of your company
Has been to your country twice

Name: Paul Dumont
From: France
Job: Trainee with a French import export company
Is working in your company for overseas experience
Has been in your country for three months

Name: Manuel Garcia
From: The Philippines
Job: Staff liaison officer in a telecommunications company
First visit to your country

Informal Leavetakings and Goodbyes

Look at this part of the conversation between Mr. Hays and Mr. Bell:

> Mr. Hays: See you tomorrow, Pete. Bye.
> Mr. Bell: OK. See you, Jim. Bye.

Note:
Mr. Hays and Mr. Bell know each other well. They use their first names and the more informal phrases *"See you (tomorrow)"* and *"Bye"* when leavetaking.

Here are some more examples of informal phrases:

		tomorrow/next week, etc.
		later.
Bye.	See you	soon.
		sometime.
		around.
	I'll be seeing you.	

Activity 8

Match the leavetaking situations on the left with the phrases on the right.

Situation

1. to a business friend after a drink after work
2. to the president of your company at the end of a formal reception
3. to your secretary at the end of the working week
4. to a regular visitor to your company at the end of the annual conference

Phrases

a. Goodbye, sir. I'll see you at the meeting on Monday.

b. Bye, see you on Monday.

c. Goodbye. It was nice meeting you again. I'll see you next time you are in town.

d. See you tomorrow. Bye.

Your Turn

Practice the following role-play in groups of three.
Take turns as A, B and C.

A
You are a visitor to B's company.
You have met B a few times before.
Respond to his or her greeting.

B introduces you to C.
Respond to C's questions.

B
You know A.
A is visiting your company.
Greet him or her.

Introduce A to your colleague C.

C
You are a colleague of B.
B is in your department.
B introduces you to A.

Ask A where he or she is from, how long he or she is planning to stay, and what he or she thinks of your town. You have to go to a meeting soon, so say goodbye to both A and B.

UNIT

3 Taking Charge

UNIT FOCUS

- **Inviting People**
- **Accepting Invitations**
- **Declining Invitations**
  Expressing Regret
- **Making Simple Arrangements**

What do you show visitors to your city/town? What do you like to do when you visit a new place?

Activity 1

Ms. Shaw is in Tokyo. She and Mr. Abe have just finished discussing a contract. Listen to the conversation and then mark the sentences true (T) or false (F).

1	Ms. Shaw has no plans for tomorrow.	T	F
2.	Mr. Abe will meet Ms. Shaw at the office.	T	F
3.	Ms. Shaw has no idea what to buy her daughter.	T	F
4.	Ms. Shaw wants to eat Western food.	T	F
5.	Neither Mr. Abe nor Ms. Shaw likes shopping.	T	F
6.	The restaurant is near the department store.	T	F

Activity 2

Listen to the conversation again and fill in the missing words and phrases.

MS. SHAW: Well, I'm glad we agree on those points.

MR. ABE: Good. We can draw up the contract on Monday.
1 ________________ tomorrow?

MS. SHAW: Not really, but I must buy some gifts for my husband and daughter.

MR. ABE: Oh, well, in that case, 2 ________________ the shopping area? I have to buy a gift for my father.

MS. SHAW: Thank you very much. 3 ________________.

MR. ABE: Good. 4 ________________ tomorrow morning about 10:30?

MS. SHAW: Yes, that's fine. So I'll see you at 10:30 tomorrow morning.
5 ________________ the lobby.

MR. ABE: Fine. Until tomorrow. 6 ________________. Goodbye.

MS. SHAW: Goodbye.

(Next day)

MR. ABE: Good morning, Ms. Shaw. How are you today?

MS. SHAW: 7 ________________, thank you. And you?

MR. ABE: Fine, thanks. 8 ________________ does your daughter like?

MS. SHAW: Well, she asked me to look for a Japanese fan.

MR. ABE: Well, we'll go to the Ginza area. There are a lot of good [9] ______________________ there.

MS. SHAW: [10] ______________________. Shall we go?

(*Later*)

MS. SHAW: Well, I'm sure my daughter will like this fan. It's beautiful.

MR. ABE: Good. Well, it's one o'clock. [11] ______________________ ______________ now?

MS. SHAW: Oh, yes, [12] ______________________. I'm pretty [13] ______ ______________.

MR. ABE: [14] ______________________ food, or [15] ______________ ______________________ Western food?

MS. SHAW: Oh, I like Japanese food, especially soba.

MR. ABE: I know an excellent soba restaurant near here. Let's try that.

(*Later*)

MS. SHAW: That was delicious. [16] ______________________ for helping me [17] ______________________________.

MR. ABE: [18] ______________________.

MS. SHAW: I [19] ______________ shopping!

MR. ABE: So do I, but I [20] __________________ for gifts.

MS. SHAW: Yes, I guess I do, too. But I [21] ______________ in a nice restaurant after!

Inviting People

Look at these phrases from the conversation:

> Would you like to come with me to the shopping area?
> Would you like to have lunch now?

Activity 3

Listen to the following short conversations and match the invitations with the pictures.

A

Conversation No.:____________________

Invitation to:______________________________

B

Conversation No.:____________________

Invitation to:______________________________

C

Conversation No.:____________________

Invitation to:______________________________

D

Conversation No.:______________________________

Invitation to:____

Now listen again. In which conversations do the people know each other well/not know each other well? Check the correct columns.

Invitation	**1**	**2**	**3**	**4**
Know each other well				
Don't know each other well				

Note:
In most business situations, use a more formal or neutral phrase like *"Would you like to. . .?"* for invitations.
Here are some more examples of invitations:

Formal	I was / We were } wondering if you would like to go for a meal?
↕	
Neutral	Would you like to go for a meal?
↕	What/How about going for a meal?
Informal	Why not come for a meal?

Activity 4

How would you invite the people in the situations below? With a partner, take turns making the invitations.

1. Invite the director of your company to dinner.
2. Invite a close colleague in your department for lunch.
3. Invite an overseas visitor to your company club for a drink.

Accepting Invitations

Activity 5

In Activity 3, the people all accepted the invitations. Listen to the conversations again. Number the phrases below to match the order of the conversations.

_____ Thank you very much. I'll look forward to that.

_____ Thanks. That's a great idea.

_____ Thanks. That sounds good.

_____ That's very kind of you. I'd like that very much.

Which of the phrases above are informal?

Note:
Remember not to mix informal with formal or neutral.

Here are some phrases for accepting invitations.
Notice that we usually thank the person first.

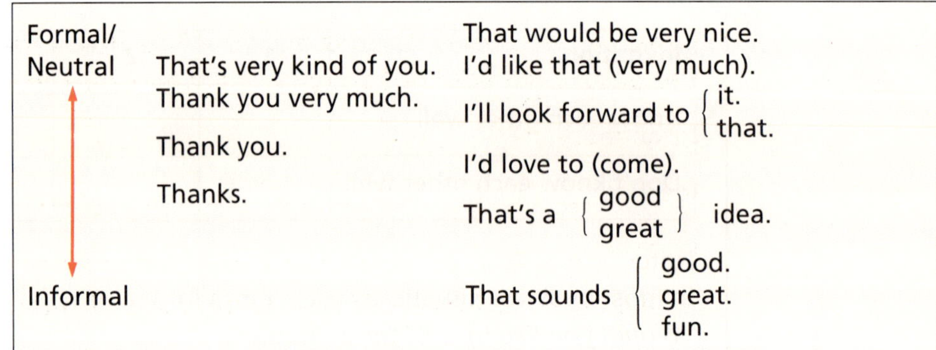

Formal/ Neutral		That would be very nice.
	That's very kind of you.	I'd like that (very much).
↑	Thank you very much.	I'll look forward to { it. / that. }
	Thank you.	I'd love to (come).
	Thanks.	That's a { good / great } idea.
↓ Informal		That sounds { good. / great. / fun. }

Activity 6

With a partner, take turns accepting these invitations.

1. How about coming for a drink after the meeting?
2. Excuse me, but we were wondering if you would like to attend the opening ceremony this afternoon?
3. How about playing a game of table tennis after lunch?
4. If you have some free time, would you like to see our display at the trade fair?

Activity 7

Work with a partner. Take turns making and accepting invitations in the following situations.
*Use **informal** (INF) or **formal** (F) language, according to the cues.*

1. Invite your boss to your birthday party on Saturday. (F)
2. Invite a close business colleague to a baseball game on Sunday. (INF)
3. Invite an overseas visitor to look around your department this afternoon. (F)
4. Your *own* idea! (INF)

Declining Invitations

Activity 8

Listen to the conversations. Which invitations are accepted (✔) and which are declined (X)? Check the spaces.

Conversation 1: ________________ Conversation 3: ________________

Conversation 2: ________________ Conversation 4: ________________

Listen to the conversations again. Write down the phrases used by the people who did not accept the invitations. The cues will help you.

(grandparents) ____

(dentist) ____

(fiance) ____

Look at these examples of how to decline an invitation:

Formal/Neutral

↕

That's very kind of you.
Thank you very much (but)
Thanks for the invitation, but

I'm afraid I can't (come, etc.)

\+ **Reason:**

. . . I have another engagement then.
. . . I'm very busy (then).
. . . I won't be here.

Thanks.

(Sorry, but) I can't (come, etc.)

\+ **Reason:**

. . . I have something else going on then.

Informal

Note:
When we cannot accept an invitation, it is polite to give a reason or an explanation why we cannot accept.

Expressing Regret

If you invite someone who declines your invitation, you can suggest something else, for example: "How about next week?" If the other person still declines, you can use an expression of regret.

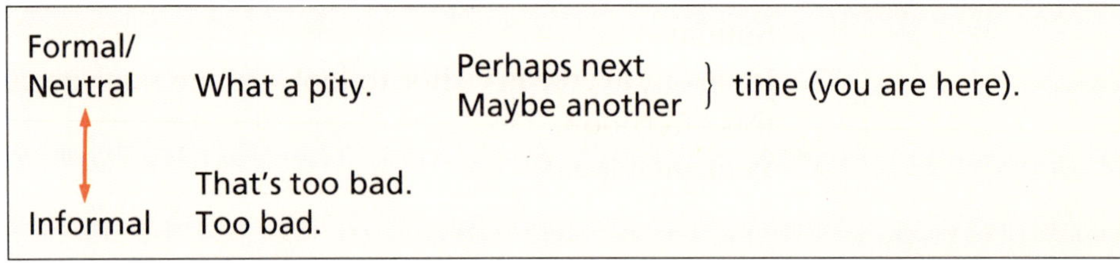

Formal/ Neutral	What a pity.	Perhaps next / Maybe another } time (you are here).
↕		
Informal	That's too bad. Too bad.	

Activity 9 *Work with a partner. Take turns declining the following invitations.*

Example:

A: Would you like to come to the office party tonight?

B: *(You have to finish a report for tomorrow morning.)*
Thank you very much, but I'm afraid I can't come.
I have to finish a report for tomorrow morning.

A	B
Would you like to visit our training center this afternoon?	You have an appointment with the overseas sales representative then.
We were wondering if you would like to come to our house on Sunday?	Your flight leaves early Sunday morning.
How about going for coffee?	You are expecting a phone call from your overseas branch.

Making Simple Arrangements

When we make invitations, we often have to make arrangements.

Look at these examples from the conversation between Ms. Shaw and Mr. Abe:

Shall I come to your hotel tomorrow morning, about 10:30?
Yes, that's fine. So I'll see you at 10:30 tomorrow morning.
I'll wait in the lobby.

The two most important things to make clear when you are making arrangements are the *meeting time* and *place*.
You can also ask direct questions: "*When/Where shall we meet?*"

Activity 10

Listen to these short conversations.
Complete the table with the correct information.

Invitation	To	Meeting Day/Time	Meeting Place
1			
2			
3			

Activity 11

Listen to the tape.
Use the phrases below to respond to Mr. Braun.
Make sure you get the correct order!

- About what time?
- Thank you very much. I'd love to come.
- So you'll meet me at 10 a.m. on Saturday just outside the hotel?
- I'll look forward to it. Goodbye.
- Yes, 10 a.m. is fine.

Activity 12

Complete the dialogue with suitable phrases.
Then practice it with a partner. Remember to check the arrangements.

A: Are you busy on Friday evening?

B: ______________________________

A: Well, my colleagues and I would like to invite you to dinner at the company club after the meeting.

B: ______________________________

A: Good. We'll meet you at the reception desk on the first floor here. We can take a taxi to the club.

B: ______________________________

A: Is 6:30 all right?

B: ______________________________
I'll look forward to it.

A: ______________________________ Goodbye.

B: ____________________

Activity 13

Work with a partner. Use the information in the table to practice making invitations, accepting invitations and making arrangements.

Invitation	Meeting Time	Meeting Place
to go sightseeing	about 1:30 this afternoon	at the main entrance of the office
to come to a cocktail party	6:00 p.m. Friday	outside the conference hall on the 3rd floor
to go to an exhibition of computer software	Wednesday afternoon	opposite the station

Now think of your own ideas for invitations, meeting times and places. Practice accepting/declining with a partner.

Your Turn

Practice the role-play with a partner. Take turns as A and B.

A
You are the site manager of one of your company's production plants.
You have just shown B around.
Invite B to dinner this evening.
You will meet B at his or her hotel at about 7:00 p.m.
You will telephone B from the reception desk when you arrive.

B
A has just shown you around his or her production plant.
A invites you to have dinner with him or her this evening.

Thank A for the invitation.

Ask A when and where to meet.

You are expecting a phone call from your head office in the USA at about 7:00 p.m.

Now do the role-play again. This time, B declines A's invitation. Give your own reasons for declining.

UNIT 4

Eating Out and Hosting

UNIT FOCUS

- Offering Food and Drink
- Accepting and Declining Food and Drink
- Describing Food and Drink
- Recommending and Suggesting
- Expressing Likes, Dislikes and Preferences
- Thanking People and Showing Appreciation

Have you ever been a guest in a restaurant abroad? Have you ever taken a foreign visitor to a restaurant in your country? What kind of food did he or she like? What did you explain to him or her?

Activity 1

Mr. Kaslan has invited Mr. Bond for lunch in a restaurant in Jakarta. Listen to the conversation and then mark the sentences true (T) or false (F).

1. Mr. Kaslan often comes to the restaurant. T F
2. Mr. Bond has often eaten Indonesian food. T F
3. Mr. Bond likes very spicy food. T F
4. Shrimp is a kind of seafood. T F
5. People often drink beer with Indonesian food. T F
6. Mr. Bond and Mr. Kaslan have coffee in the restaurant. T F

Activity 2

Listen to the conversation again and complete the missing words or phrases.

MR. KASLAN: Have a seat, Mr. Bond.

MR. BOND: This is a nice restaurant.

MR. KASLAN: Yes, I often bring guests here. I like the food very much. Now, [1]____________________?

MR. BOND: Well, I've never eaten Indonesian food before. What [2]____________________?

MR. KASLAN: OK, let's look at the menu. [3]____________________ hot, spicy food?

MR. BOND: Well, yes, but I don't really like *very* spicy food.

MR. KASLAN: In that case, [4]____________________ some sate ayam. That's small pieces of chicken, grilled on a skewer. It comes with a special sauce.

MR. BOND: That sounds good.

MR. KASLAN: [5]____________________ seafood?

MR. BOND: Oh, yes, [6]____________________.

MR. KASLAN: Well, [7]____________________ some sambal goreng udang? That's shrimp fried in a coconut sauce. And we'll have some vegetables, too. Gado-gado should be nice.

MR. BOND: What's gado-gado?

MR. KASLAN: It's a mixed vegetable salad with a peanut sauce. And we'll have some plain boiled rice.

MR. BOND: [8] ______________________ .

MR. KASLAN: [9] ________________________________ to drink?

MR. BOND: Yes, please. What goes best with sate ayam and udang?

MR. KASLAN: [10] ______________________ Bintang beer. We don't usually drink anything stronger with our meals.

MR. BOND: Fine. Do you use chopsticks in Indonesia, Mr. Kaslan?

MR. KASLAN: Oh, no, we use a fork and a spoon. Well, let's order.

(*Later*)

MR. KASLAN: [11] ______________ , Mr. Bond.

(*Later*)

MR. KASLAN: [12] __________________ some fruit?

MR. BOND: Well, I've had plenty to eat, but [13] ______________________

______________________ ?

MR. KASLAN: [14] ________________ some tropical fruit? Rambutan is very refreshing.

MR. BOND: Mmm, they look interesting. How do you eat them?

MR. KASLAN: Press them at the top. The skin will break, so you can remove it. Then just bite into it. But be careful – there's a big pit inside.

MR. BOND: [15] __________________________________ . They taste a bit like lychees.

MR. KASLAN: Would you like [16] ________________ ?

MR. BOND: Oh, no, thank you, [17] ___________________ .

That was a delicious meal. Thank you very much.

And [18] _______________________ all the dishes to me.

MR. KASLAN: My pleasure. I'm glad you enjoyed it. We'll have some real Javanese coffee in a coffee shop near here.

Offering Food and Drink

Look at these phrases from the conversation:

What would you like to eat? How about some sambal goreng udang? Would you like some fruit? Why not try some tropical fruit? Would you like any more beer?

Activity 3 *Match the offers on the left with the responses on the right.*

Offers	**Responses**
1. Would you like anything more to eat?	a. Yes, that sounds good.
2. Would you like some wine?	b. No, thank you. I don't really like cheese.
3. How about some cheese?	c. Yes, please. Just a small glass.
4. Why not try the chicken?	d. No, thank you. I've had plenty to eat.

Accepting and Declining Food and Drink

In Activity 3, which offers were accepted and which were declined?

Here are some more phrases for accepting or declining offers:

Accepting	**Declining**
Yes, please.	No, thank you. I've had plenty to { eat. / drink. }
Yes, please. That sounds { good. / delicious. / nice. }	No, thanks. I don't { really like . . . / eat . . . / drink . . . }
Yes, thank you. { Just a little. / Not too much. }	No, thanks. I can't { eat . . . / drink . . . }

Note:

When we decline offers of food or drink, we often give a reason.
It is a good idea to let people know if there are some kinds of food or drink you dislike or cannot have.

Activity 4 *Practice offering and accepting or declining the food and drinks in the pictures below.*

Example:

A: Would you like { some tea? / some potatoes? } B: Yes, please. Just { a little. / a few. }

A: Would you like an omelette? B: No, thank you.

Describing Food and Drink

Mr. Bond had never eaten Indonesian food, so Mr. Kaslan described some dishes to him.

Activity 5

Look back at Activity 2. How does Mr. Kaslan describe these dishes?

1. sate ayam
2. sambal goreng udang
3. gado-gado

Underline the descriptions.

Here are some more phrases to help you explain food:

It's a kind of / That's { soup/sauce. / fish/meat dish. / vegetable/fruit. / cake. / drink. }

It's { grilled. / (deep-)fried. / (stir-)fried. / boiled/steamed. / baked/roasted. }

It tastes { salty. / sweet. / sour. / hot. / bitter. / bland. / spicy. / like ... (something else). }

It's served with a sauce.
It comes with a sauce.

Activity 6

Write the names of three or four typical dishes in your country. Explain them to your partner.

Recommending and Suggesting

Activity 7

Look back at Activity 2. Read the dialogue and complete the table with suitable responses or questions.

Mr. Bond	**Mr. Kaslan**
What would you recommend? →	
? →	I'd recommend Bintang beer.
What do you suggest? →	

Activity 8

Match the food and drinks listed below.
Practice asking for and giving recommendations.

Example:

A: What drink goes best with steak?

B: I('d) recommend red wine (with steak).

Drink

vodka Chinese green tea sake red wine beer

Food

1. coq au vin
2. curry
3. caviar

4. sweet and sour fish
5. sashimi

Do you all agree with the recommendations?
Now use your own list from Activity 6. What food and drink would you recommend to a visitor to your country?
With a partner, practice asking for and making recommendations.

Activity 9 *Mr. Gomez has invited Mr. Balendra to a Mexican restaurant. Complete the dialogue with suitable phrases. Then take turns practicing it with a partner.*

MR. GOMEZ: So, Mr. Balendra,

1________________________________?

MR. BALENDRA: Oh, I don't really know much about Mexican food.

2____?

MR. GOMEZ: Well, 3______________________ spicy food?

MR. BALENDRA: Yes, 4__________________________.

MR. GOMEZ: Good. In that case, 5______________________ guacamole and nachos to start with, followed by enchiladas and hot sauce.

MR. BALENDRA: That 6______________________.

MR. GOMEZ: 7____?

MR. BALENDRA: What do you suggest?

MR. GOMEZ: 8____________________________ tequila?

MR. BALENDRA: Fine. 9______________________ the guacamole?

MR. GOMEZ: Just dip the nachos into the guacamole and eat them with your fingers.

(*Later*)

MR. GOMEZ: Would you like anything more to eat or drink?

MR. BALENDRA: No, thank you. 10__________________.

MR. GOMEZ: Did you enjoy your first Mexican meal?

MR. BALENDRA: 11____.

MR. GOMEZ: My pleasure. I'm glad you liked it.

Expressing Likes, Dislikes and Preferences

Activity 10

Look at these questions and answers from the dialogue.

Mr. Kaslan	**Mr. Bond**
Do you like hot, spicy food?	Well, yes, but I don't really like *very* spicy food.
Do you like seafood?	Oh, yes. I like it very much.

What would Mr. Kaslan have said if Mr. Bond's second answer had been negative? Discuss with the class.

Activity 11

Listen to the two conversations.
Which one do you like better? Why?
Discuss your answer with the rest of the class.

When we express likes or dislikes, we often show the *degree* of liking or disliking.

Look at some more examples:

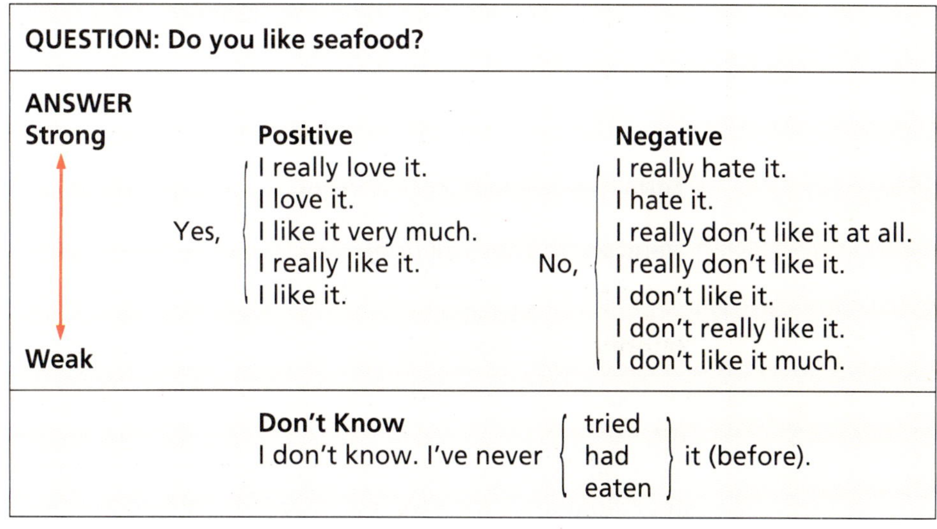

QUESTION: Do you like seafood?

ANSWER		**Positive**		**Negative**
Strong	Yes,	I really love it.	No,	I really hate it.
		I love it.		I hate it.
		I like it very much.		I really don't like it at all.
		I really like it.		I really don't like it.
		I like it.		I don't like it.
				I don't really like it.
Weak				I don't like much.

Don't Know
I don't know. I've never { tried / had / eaten } it (before).

Note:
When you are a guest and someone is paying for your meal, it is not polite to say "I really hate _____".
It is better to say "I'm afraid I don't really like _____ very much."

Activity 12 *Look at the list of food and drink in Activity 8.*
With a partner, take turns asking and answering about your food and drink likes/dislikes. Express the degree of liking/disliking.
Say what you prefer.

Note:
The phrases above can also be used to express likes and dislikes for other things: sports, hobbies, interests, etc.

Thanking People and Showing Appreciation

At the end of their meal, Mr. Bond thanks Mr. Kaslan. How does Mr. Kaslan respond? Look back at Activity 2. Underline what they say.

Look at these examples:

Thank you (very much) for the meal. It was { delicious. / wonderful. / great.

Thanks for { explaining the dishes to me. / helping me with the menu.

Here are some examples of responses to "thanks":

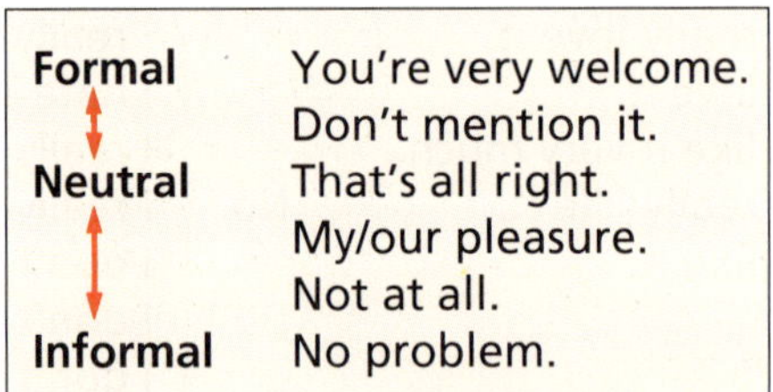

Formal	You're very welcome.
↕	Don't mention it.
Neutral	That's all right.
↕	My/our pleasure.
	Not at all.
Informal	No problem.

Note:
These phrases can also be used for thanking/showing appreciation in other situations, for example: thanking people for a weekend, a sight-seeing tour, and so on.

Activity 13

Match the situations on the left with the responses on the right.

Situation	**Response**
1. after an evening at a concert	a. Thank you very much for the tour. It was very interesting.
2. after a picnic in the country	b. Thank you very much for the invitation. It was really enjoyable.
3. after a sightseeing tour of the city	c. Thanks for everything. It was a lovely day.

Activity 14

With a partner, take turns thanking/showing appreciation and responding in the following situations. Take turns as the host and guest.

1. after a day at the beach
2. after a visit to the museum
3. after a weekend at your host's home
4. after a game of tennis at your host's club

Your Turn

Practice the role-play with a partner. Take turns as A and B.

A	B
This is your first visit to B's country. You are free this afternoon and evening. B invites you to lunch. You accept. At the restaurant, you don't know what to choose. Ask about the dishes on the menu. Ask B to recommend something	This is A's first visit to your country. Invite A to lunch. Ask A if he or she is free this afternoon. At the restaurant, A doesn't know what to choose. Explain the dishes on the menu. Recommend something when A asks.
(When the meal is over) Thank B for the meal.	(When the meal is over) Respond to A's thanks.

UNIT

5 Getting to Know You

UNIT FOCUS

- **Starting a Conversation**
- **Continuing a Conversation — More Small Talk Topics**
- **Ending a Conversation Showing Interest (1)**

Have you ever attended an international conference? Where? What was the conference theme? Did you talk to any of the delegates in English? What language(s) did the conference presenters use?

Activity 1

Mr. Wang and Mr. Hakim are at an international conference in Singapore. Listen to the conversation and then mark the sentences true (T) or false (F).

1. Mr. Wang works for a Japanese company. T F
2. Mr. Wang has never been to Malaysia. T F
3. Mr. Hakim has lived in Kuala Lumpur for two years. T F
4. Mr. Hakim's wife liked Kota Kinabalu. T F
5. Mr. Wang often goes to Japan. T F
6. Mr. Hakim and Mr. Wang want to hear the same speaker. T F

Activity 2

Listen to the conversation again and fill in the missing words or phrases.

MR. WANG: [1]____________________ so far, Mr. Hakim?

MR. HAKIM: Yes, I've learned some new things today. And [2]____________________, Mr. Wang?

MR. WANG: [3]________________ in Taiwan. [4]________________ Ace Computer Company in Taipei. It's a subsidiary of Ace Electronics in Japan.

MR. HAKIM: I see, and [5]________________?

MR. WANG: I'm a systems analyst. Most of the time, I'm in Taipei, but I usually go to Tokyo once a year to visit our head office.

MR. HAKIM: [6]________________?

MR. WANG: No, I live just outside the city. It's much quieter. And what about you? [7]________________?

MR. HAKIM: I'm an engineer with the Malaysian Television Authority.

MR. WANG: [8]________________?

MR. HAKIM: In Kuala Lumpur, but I used to live in Kota Kinabalu.

MR. WANG: That's in Sabah, isn't it?

MR. HAKIM: That's right. I was transferred to Kuala Lumpur two years ago.

MR. WANG: [9]________________?

MR. HAKIM: Yes, I liked it very much. [10]______________________________

______________________________. But I'm afraid my wife didn't enjoy it at all! So she is very happy now in Kuala Lumpur.

MR. WANG: I visited Kuala Lumpur last year on a business trip. But I didn't see very much because I only had one day free, and it rained!

MR. HAKIM: Oh, that's too bad! Well, if you get the chance to visit again, my wife and I will be happy to show you around.

MR. WANG: [11]______________________________. Thank you.

MR. HAKIM: Well, [12]______________________________ in a few minutes. Which talk are you going to now, Mr. Wang?

MR. WANG: I'd like to hear the talk by Dr. Ogawa. It's in room 20.

MR. HAKIM: I'm going to room 3. [13]______________________________, Mr. Wang.

MR. WANG: Yes, [14]______________________________. I hope

[15]______________________________. Goodbye.

MR. HAKIM: [16]____________________.

Starting a Conversation

Look at these phrases:

> Are you enjoying the conference so far, Mr. Hakim?
> And where exactly are you from, Mr. Wang?
> I see, and what do you do?
> Do you live in Taipei?
> What's your job?
> Where do you live?

Activity 3

Listen to the two conversations. The two speakers are attending an international conference in Seoul.

a. Which conversation is better? Why?
b. Make a list of any situations where you might have to make "small talk" with people from other countries.
c. What would you talk about?

Activity 4

*Look at the **situations** on the left. Match them with suitable **opening comments** on the right.*

Situation	Opening Comment
1. At the beginning of a site tour of a factory.	a. Are you enjoying the seminar?
2. At a dinner celebrating the 10th anniversary of a multinational company.	b. What do you think of the new recruiting policy?
3. At a meeting of company representatives from overseas branches to discuss how to attract new staff.	c. Is this your first visit to this site?
4. At the coffee break during an intensive technical writing seminar.	d. The opening speech was very funny. What did you think?

Activity 5

Listen to the conversation between Mr. Davies and Mr. Stein. Circle the questions that Mr. Davies asks Mr. Stein. Number them in the correct order.

Questions:

What did you think of the seminar?	Where do you live?
Do you work in Basel, too?	Do you live in Basel?
What do you do?	Where exactly in Switzerland?
What's your job?	What company do you work for?
Are you enjoying the seminar?	Where are you from?

Note:
If you want to continue a conversation after you have started it, you can ask the other person about him or herself. Of course, you must also be ready to tell him or her about yourself.

Activity 6

Work with a partner. Practice asking and answering questions about your work, where you live, etc.

Activity 7

Listen to the conversation. Three people are talking about themselves. Complete the table below with the correct information.

Name	Job	Company	Work-place	Residence
Mai Manoon				Lantau Island
Paul Slade		Trident Photocopiers		
Mike Drew	Advertising Director			

Activity 8

Imagine you are in the two situations below.
Write down some opening comments for each situation and questions that you could ask to continue the conversations.
Work with a partner. Take turns starting the conversation.

Situation 1

You have just listened to a speech by your company's president at the international headquarters in Chicago. You want to start a conversation with an American sitting next to you.

Situation 2

You are touring the assembly line of an overseas factory which produces automobile parts for your company. You want to talk to a foreman.

Continuing a Conversation — More Small Talk Topics

Look at these phrases from the conversation between Mr. Wang and Mr. Hakim:

Did you like Sabah?
Yes, I liked it very much. But I'm afraid my wife didn't enjoy it at all.
I visited Kuala Lumpur last year on a business trip.
Well, if you get the chance to visit again, my wife and I will be happy to show you around.

Note:
After you have asked someone about his or her work, where he or she lives, etc., you can continue the conversation by asking other kinds of questions. Mr. Hakim and Mr. Wang continued the conversation by talking about their experiences.

Activity 9

Listen to the four conversations and try to identify the small talk topic. Write your answers in the spaces.

Conversation	1	2	3	4
Topic				

Activity 10

Write a list of small talk topics which you could use when meeting people at any kind of international conference, seminar, business lunch, etc. How could you start the conversation? Write your topics and starting phrases in the table.

Example:
Topic: The keynote speech

Starting phrase: I enjoyed the keynote speaker. Do you know him?

Topic	Starting Phrase
1. ____________	____________________________
2. ____________	____________________________
3. ____________	____________________________

Work with a partner or in small groups. Use your topics and starting phrases to start and continue a conversation for at least 10 minutes.

Ending a Conversation

Look at these phrases from Mr. Wang and Mr. Hakim's conversation:

Well, the next session begins in a few minutes, Mr. Wang.
It was very nice meeting you, Mr. Wang.
It was nice meeting you, too. I hope we'll see each other again.

Note:
When we want to end a conversation, we usually give a "signal" to the other person. The "signal" lets him or her know that the conversation will end soon.

Question:
What was Mr. Hakim's "signal"?

Activity 11

Listen to the two conversations. One of the speakers wants to end the conversation.

1. Which conversation is better? Why?
2. In the good conversation, what "signal" does the first speaker use?

Note:
It is important to *give a reason* for ending a conversation.

The "signal" phrase that shows you want to end a conversation is often a *reason*. In the conversation between Mr. Wang and Mr. Hakim, the reason was that *the next session began in a few minutes*.

Activity 12

1. *Listen to these "ends" of conversations and match them with the correct reasons below.*

Conversation	**Reason**
1.	a. The first speaker has to catch a flight.
2.	b. The first speaker has to write a report for tomorrow.
3.	c. The first speaker has to meet his boss for dinner.

2. *Now write the "signal" phrases in the spaces.*

Conversation 1: ______________________________

Conversation 2: ______________________________

Conversation 3: ______________________________

Note:
It is usual to preface your reason for ending a conversation with phrases like those you wrote above.

Here are some examples:

I'm sorry, but I have to I'm afraid . . . I'll have to I really have to	{ go leave }	(you) now.

Showing Interest (1)

When you give a "signal" phrase to end a conversation, you often also show the other person that:

(a) you were pleased to have met him or her

and (b) you hope to see him or her again in the future.

Look at these examples:

a	b
It was (very) nice meeting you. It was nice talking to you. I enjoyed talking to you. I enjoyed meeting you.	I hope we'll see each other again. I hope we'll meet again. I'm sure we'll see each other again (soon). I'll see you after the meeting.

Activity 13

Work with a partner. Take turns to end a conversation using the cues. Make sure to give a response.

1. You have to make an urgent phone call.
2. You have to go to a reception for a visiting client.
3. You have to catch a train back to the city.
4. You have to read a long report for a meeting this evening.

Activity 14

Make a list of other reasons why you end conversations. Practice some of your ideas with a partner.

Your Turn

Practice the following role-play with your partner. Take turns as A and B.

A	B
You are attending an inter-national seminar in your own country. You meet B and start a conversation with him or her. Find out where B comes from, what B does, what company B works for. Keep the conversation going.	You are attending an international seminar in A's country. Answer A's questions. Keep the conversation going. You have to see one of the seminar organizers, so end the conversation after you have answered all of A's questions.

UNIT

6 Getting Personal

UNIT FOCUS

- **Showing Someone Around**
  Offers and Suggestions
  Showing Interest (2)
- **Making and Responding to Simple Requests**
- **Home Visits: Being a Good Guest/Host**
  Asking for/Giving Permission
  Understanding Customs

Have you ever taken a foreign visitor sightseeing? Have you ever invited a foreign visitor to your home or been a guest in someone's home in another country? Were there any problems?

Activity 1

Mr. Sato has just finished lunch with Mr. Barr, a golf-club manufacturer, in St. Andrews, Scotland.
Listen to the conversation and mark the sentences true (T) or false (F).

1. Mr. Sato will be working after lunch. T F
2. Mr. Sato is a member of the Royal and Ancient Golf Club. T F
3. Mr. Sato can't take photographs in the chapel. T F
4. St. Rule's Tower is not safe. T F
5. Mr. Sato takes some photographs from the top of the tower. T F
6. Mr. Barr knows a lot about his town. T F

Activity 2

Listen to the conversation again and fill in the missing words or phrases.

MR. SATO: That was a delicious meal, Mr. Barr. Thank you very much.

MR. BARR: My pleasure. Do you have any plans for this afternoon?

MR. SATO: No, not really.

MR. BARR: Well, in that case, [1]______________________________ the town? St. Andrews is quite an interesting place.

MR. SATO: [2]______________________________ . I'd love to do some sightseeing.

MR. BARR: Well, if you're ready, let's go.

That building in front of us is the Royal and Ancient Golf Club, but you probably know that already.

MR. SATO: Yes, it's quite well-known in Japan. [3]____________________ ____________________ some time?

MR. BARR: Yes, [4]____________________ . I'm a club member. I'll take you there tomorrow if you like. We'll go along this street. Now on the right is one of the older parts of the university. Let's go in this way. This is called the "Quad."

MR. SATO: [5]______________ . How old is the university?

MR. BARR: Well, it was founded in 1412 AD, so it's over 500 years old.

MR. SATO: How interesting. [6]____________________ over there?

MR. BARR: That's the university chapel, a church for the students.

MR. SATO: [7]____________________ I take photographs inside?

MR. BARR: [8]______________ .
Now let's go out this way and we'll go to the cathedral.

MR. SATO: Is [9]______________________________ ?

MR. BARR: No, I'm afraid it's mostly in ruins now.

MR. SATO: [10]______________________________ , isn't it? What's that tower?

MR. BARR: St. Rule's Tower. You get a wonderful view from the roof.

MR. SATO: [11]______________________________ ?

MR. BARR: I'm [12]________________ . Visitors aren't allowed to go up because the stairs are broken. It's too dangerous.

MR. SATO: What a pity.

MR. BARR: I'll take you down to the castle now.

MR. SATO: [13]______________________ built?

MR. BARR: I'm not sure, but I think it's older than the university.

(Later)

Well, Mr. Sato, are you tired? [14]____________________________ ?

MR. SATO: Well, yes, I am beginning to feel a bit tired.

MR. BARR: Would [15]____ ?

MR. SATO: Oh, thank you, but [16]______________________________ . It's not far. [17]______________________________ tour. Thank you.

MR. BARR: I'm glad [18]______________________. I'll call you tomorrow. Goodbye.

MR. SATO: Fine. Goodbye and [19]___________________ .

Showing Someone Around

Offers and Suggestions

Look at these phrases from the conversation:

Would you like me to show you around the town?
That's very kind of you. I'd love to do some sightseeing.
Would you like me to drive you back to your hotel?
Thank you, but please don't bother. It's not far.

Here are some more useful phrases:

Would you like me to Should I	get you a coffee? call a taxi? arrange your accommodation?

Activity 3

Match the situations on the left with the offers on the right.

Situation	Offer
1. Your overseas visitor needs to get to the airport quickly.	a. Would you like me to get you the company brochure?
2. You and your visitor have just returned from a four-hour tour of a factory.	b. Would you like me to call a taxi for you?
3. Your visitor wants to know more about your company's history.	c. Would you like to take a rest before we see the administrative section?

How would you respond to the above offers/suggestions? Work with a partner. Take turns making and responding to the offers/suggestions.

Here are some examples:

Accepting	**Declining**
(Yes,) that would be good. / nice. / lovely. Thank you very much. That's very kind of you.	(No,) thank you. That's not necessary. Thank you, but please don't bother.

Note:
We often give a reason when we decline an offer/suggestion.

Activity 4

Listen to the offers/suggestions.
Respond to them. Give a reason if you decline.
(✓ = accept ✗ = decline)
Listen to the example.

1. ✗ (you already have a ticket)

2. ✓

3. ✗ (you have too many meetings tomorrow)

Listen to the tape again. Write down the offers/suggestions. With a partner, practice making and responding to them.

Showing Interest (2)

When he was being shown around St. Andrews, Mr. Sato showed interest by asking questions and making comments.

Activity 5

Look at Activity 2 again. Underline Mr. Sato's questions and comments.

Note:
If someone is showing you around, it is important to show interest by asking questions and making comments. This shows that you are paying attention.

Even if you are not very interested or are tired, try to respond to your host's explanations. If you are the host/guide, it is terrible to get no reaction from your guest!

Here are some more phrases to show you are interested:

This That	is	lovely. beautiful. fascinating. interesting. wonderful.	What a/an	lovely beautiful fascinating interesting wonderful	museum. building. painting. view. tour. story.

Activity 6

Draw a map of a local place that you like and would show to a visitor on foot.
Work with a partner. Take turns as the host and the visitor. The host should point out places of interest. The visitor should show interest.

Making and Responding to Simple Requests

During his tour of St. Andrews, Mr. Sato wanted to know if he could do some things.

Look at these examples from the conversation:

> Would it be possible to see inside some time?
> Is it all right if I take photographs inside?
> Can we go up to the roof?

Note:
When you are a guest or a visitor, you often need to make requests or ask for permission to do things, especially if you are not sure of local customs.

Activity 7

Listen. Mr. Sato is making some requests during his stay in St. Andrews. Where do the conversations take place? Write your answers below.

1. ______________________ 2. ______________________

3. ______________________ 4. ______________________

How does Mr. Sato make his requests? Listen again. Write what he says. The first one is done for you.

Request 1: Could I have a pot of coffee and some sandwiches, please?

(Response): ______________________

Request 2: ______________________ a taxi for me, please?

(Response):

____

Request 3: ______________________ my return flight to Osaka, please?

(Response): ______________________

Request 4: ______________________ to send a fax to Japan?

(Response): ______________________

How do the people respond to Mr. Sato's requests? Listen again and write the responses in the spaces.

Now look at these phrases:

	Request	**Positive Response**	**Negative Response**
Formal	Would it be possible to . . . ?	Certainly, { sir. / ma'am. }	I'm afraid / I'm sorry, but } that's not possible.
↕	Could / Can } I/We . . .?	(Yes,) Of course.	
Informal		That's no problem.	I'm afraid not.

Note:

Sir/ma'am are usually used only by people in service situations. When people respond negatively to a request, they often give a reason or an explanation why the request is not possible. What reasons did people give in Activity 7?

Activity 8 *Match the requests on the left with the responses on the right.*

Requests

1. Would it be possible to leave my bags here until 8:00 p.m.?
2. Can you type this report for me before 5:00 p.m., please?
3. Would it be possible to change our appointment to next Monday?

Responses

a. I'm sorry, but I have to go to the doctor's at 4:00 p.m.

b. I'm afraid not. I'll be on vacation all next week.

c. Yes, of course. I'll put them in the left luggage store-room.

Home Visits: Being a Good Guest/Host

Asking for/Giving Permission

Activity 9 *Mr. Barr invited Mr. Sato to his home for lunch. Mr. Sato asked if he could do certain things. Listen to the conversation.*

1. *Make a list of the things he asked to do. Was he given permission? Discuss with a partner.*
2. *How did Mr. Sato ask for permission? Listen again and write the phrases.*

Now look at these phrases:

	Asking for Permission	Giving Permission	Refusing Permission
Formal	Would / Do } you mind if I smoke?	No, I { wouldn't / don't } mind (at all).	I'm sorry, (but) / I'm afraid } I'm allergic to smoke.
		No, not at all.	
Neutral	Is it all right if I smoke?	Yes, { it is. / it's all right.	I'm sorry, but it's not all right.
		Yes, { of course. / certainly.	
Informal	May / Can } I smoke?	Yes, go ahead. Sure. Fine. OK. No problem.	(No,) I'm afraid not.

Note:
When we refuse permission, it is polite to give a reason. A direct refusal ("Yes, I do mind if you smoke.") is not very polite. It may offend the other person.

Do you mind if I smoke?

Activity 10

Match the questions on the left with the responses on the right.

Requests for Permission	**Responses**
1. Do you mind if I open the window?	a. No, not at all. It *is* very hot in here.
2. Would it be all right if I took off my jacket?	b. Of course. It's at the end of the hall.
3. May I use the bathroom?	c. I'm sorry, but I have a terrible cold. Would you mind keeping it closed?

Activity 11

You have invited a foreign visitor to spend a weekend at your home. Listen to his questions. Write the correct number next to each question as you hear them.

______ Could I have an extra pillow, please?

______ Can I help you with the dishes?

______ Would you mind if I took a shower now?

______ Do you mind if I watch the news on TV?

How would you answer these questions? Work with a partner. Take turns asking and answering.

Understanding Customs

Why did Mr. Sato ask if he could take off his shoes?

Note:
When you visit people in their homes in another country, it is easy to seem impolite if you do not know the customs.

Activity 12

Look at the list. What is normal or not normal when visiting homes in these parts of the world?

Asia **Southeast Asia** **North America** **Africa**
South America **The Middle East** **Europe**

1. Shaking hands
2. Arriving early
3. Bringing a gift
4. Wearing short pants
5. Making noises when eating
6. Removing your shoes
7. Eating with your fingers
8. Arriving more than 30 minutes late
9. (Men) Speaking to female members of the family

What advice would you give to a foreigner making a home visit in your country? Discuss with your partner.

Your Turn

Practice the role-play with a partner. Take turns as A and B.

A
You and B work for the same multi-national company. This is your first visit to B's country. B has invited you to his or her home for a meal. None of B's family speaks English. Respond to B's greeting and introductions to his or her family.
Show interest in B's family, and request to do some things.
Show your appreciation.

B
You and A work for the same multi-national company. This is A's first visit to your country. You have invited A to your home for a meal. None of your family speaks English. Greet A and introduce him or her to your family.
Respond to A's requests.

Answer Key and Transcripts

Unit 1

Activity 1

1. T 2. F 3. F 4. T 5. T 6. T

Activity 2

MR. ANDO: [1]*Good morning.* [2]*My name is* Ken Ando. I'm the head of sales from the Tokyo office. I have an appointment with Ms. Tod.

RECEPTIONIST: Oh, yes, Mr. Ando. [3]*Good morning.* Ms. Tod is expecting you. Please go right in.

MR. ANDO: Thank you. (*Sound of a knock at the door.*) [4]*Good morning,* Ms. Tod. [5]*I'm Ken Ando from* Tokyo.

MS. TOD: Ah, yes, please come in, Mr. Ando.

MR. ANDO: [6]*How do you do,* Ms. Tod? It's [7]*nice to meet* you.

MS. TOD: [8]*How do you do, Mr. Ando?* [9]*It's nice to meet you,* too. Welcome to San Francisco. [10]*I hope you enjoy* your visit.

MR. ANDO: Thank you. [11]*I'm sure* I will.

MS. TOD: Please, take a seat. [12]*Would you like* some tea or coffee?

MR. ANDO: Thank you, I'd like coffee, please. Black with no sugar.

MS. TOD: *(Speaks into intercom.)* Ms. Hind, could we have two coffees, please? One black with no sugar, and one with cream and no sugar. Well, Mr. Ando, [13]*when did you arrive?*

MR. ANDO: Yesterday morning.

MS. TOD: [14]*How was your flight?*

MR. ANDO: [15]*Fine, thanks.* I stopped off in Hawaii for a day to visit some friends, so I didn't have a long flight.

MS. TOD: That's good. And [16]*how is your hotel?*

MR. ANDO: It's [17]*very comfortable,* and very [18]*convenient.* It's right next to a bus stop.

MS. TOD: Ah, that's very important in San Francisco!

Activity 3

1. b 3. c 2. a

Activity 5

b.
Suitable Questions to ask an American: 1, 2, 4, 9, 10
Unsuitable Questions to ask an American: 3, 5, 6, 7, 8, 11

Activity 6

Suggested answers:

The Flight/Journey

How was your / Did you have a good { flight? / trip? / journey? }

Plans

How long { are you planning to stay / will you be staying } in (country's name)?

Activity 6

The Visitor's Country
Which part of (visitor's country) are you from?
Where {do you live / are you from} in (visitor's country)?

The Weather
What {is / was} the weather like {in / when you left} (visitor's country)?
How was the weather in (visitor's country)?

Previous Visits to your Country
Is this your first visit to (country)?
Have you visited (country) before?

Accommodation
How is your hotel?
Is your hotel OK?
I hope your hotel is all right?

Activity 7

Suggested answers:

MS. THOMAS: Welcome to New York, Mr. Santos. I hope your flight was OK?
MR. SANTOS: [1]*Yes, it was fine, thank you.*
MS. THOMAS: Is this your first visit to the United States?
MR. SANTOS: [2]*No, I was here two years ago.*
MS. THOMAS: Oh, where were you?
MR. SANTOS: [3]*I was in Miami on vacation.*
MS. THOMAS: I see. Well, you'll find New York quite different! [4]*Where are you from in the Philippines, Mr. Santos?*
MR. SANTOS: I'm from San Fernando.
MS. THOMAS: [5]*Where exactly is that?*
MR. SANTOS: It's north of Manila.
MS. THOMAS: Ah, I see. [6]*How long will you be staying in New York?*
MR. SANTOS: I'll probably be staying for four days. I have to go to Washington next week.
MS. THOMAS: Well, [7]*I hope you enjoy your visit!*
MR. SANTOS: Thank you, I'm sure I will!

Activity 8

MS. TOD: Well, [1]*it's been very nice meeting you, Mr. Ando.* I hope to see you again on Wednesday.
MR. ANDO: [2]*It was nice meeting you, too, Ms. Tod.* I'll see you on Wednesday. Thank you. [3]*Goodbye.*
MS. TOD: Goodbye.

Unit 2

Activity 1

1. T 2. T 3. F 4. T 5. F 6. F

Activity 2

MR. BELL: Oh, [1]*hello*, Mr. Moon. It's [2]*nice to see you again.*
MR. MOON: [3]*Hello*, Mr. Bell. I'm pleased to see you again, too. [4]*How are you?*
MR. BELL: I'm [5]*very well*, thank you. And you?
MR. MOON: I'm fine. And [6]*how is your family?*
MR. BELL: They're all very well, thank you. What about your family? [7]*How are they?*
MR. MOON: They're also very well.
MR. BELL: I'm glad to hear it. And you're still living in Pusan?
MR. MOON: Yes, but we moved to a bigger house last year.
MR. BELL: That's nice. Oh, there's my colleague, Mr. Hays. [8]*Hello*, Jim! Come and join us.
MR. HAYS: Hello, Pete! How [9]*are you doing?*
MR. BELL: Fine, thanks. Let me [10]*introduce* Mr. Moon. He's from Korean Paper Corporation. Mr. Moon, [11]*may I introduce* Mr. Hays? He's a [12]*colleague of mine* in the Research and Development Department.
MR. MOON: [13]*How do you do*, Mr. Hays? It's nice to meet you.
MR. HAYS: How do you do, Mr. Moon? [14]*It's nice to meet you, too.* Where [15]*are you from in Korea*, Mr. Moon?
MR. MOON: I'm from Pusan. Do you know it?
MR. HAYS: No, but I visited Seoul two years ago. [16]*Is this your first visit* to Canada?
MR. MOON: Yes, it is.
MR. HAYS: What do you think of it?
MR. MOON: Well, it's quite different from Korea. There's so much space!
MR. HAYS: [17]*How long are you planning to stay?*
MR. MOON: Well, my visit is for a week, but I may stay a few extra days.
MR. HAYS: I hope you enjoy your visit.
MR. MOON: Thank you. I'm sure I will.
MR. HAYS: [18]*Excuse me*, but I have to speak to my supervisor. It was nice meeting you, Mr. Moon.
MR. MOON: Nice meeting you, too. Goodbye.
MR. HAYS: [19]*See you tomorrow*, Pete. [20]*Bye.*
MR. BELL: OK, [21]*see you, Jim.* Bye.

Activity 4

Suggested responses are in italics.

1. GREETING: Hello. It's nice to see you again. How have you been?
   RESPONSE: *I'm pleased to see you again, too. I've been very well, thank you.*
2. GREETING: Hi! How is it going?
   RESPONSE: *Fine, thanks.*
3. GREETING: Hello. I'm pleased to see you again. How are things?
   RESPONSE: *It's good to see you again, too. Not too bad, thanks.*
4. GREETING: Hi! It's good to see you again. How are you?
   RESPONSE: *Nice to see you, too. I'm fine.*
5. GREETING: Hi! How are you doing?
   RESPONSE: *Not too bad, thanks.*

Activity 5

Suggested responses:
1. I'm (name) from (company). How do you do, Mr. Schmidt.
2. Hello (Pete). It's nice to see you again. How have you been?
3. Hi, (Jim), how's it going?

Activity 8

1. d 2. a 3. b 4. c

Unit 3

Activity 1

1. T 2. F 3. F 4. F 5. T 6. T

Activity 2

MS. SHAW: Well, I'm glad we agree on those points.
MR. ABE: Good. We can draw up the contract on Monday. [1]*Do you have any plans for* tomorrow?
MS. SHAW: Not really, but I must buy some gifts for my husband and daughter.
MR. ABE: Oh, well, in that case, [2]*would you like to come with me to* the shopping area? I have to buy a gift for my father.
MS. SHAW: Thank you very much. [3]*That would be very nice.*
MR. ABE: Good. [4]*Should I come to your hotel* tomorrow morning about 10:30?
MS. SHAW: Yes, that's fine. So I'll see you at 10:30 tomorrow morning. [5]*I'll wait in* the lobby.
MR. ABE: Fine. Until tomorrow. [6]*Have a nice evening.* Goodbye.
MS. SHAW: Goodbye.

(*Next Day*)
MR. ABE: Good morning, Ms. Shaw. How are you today?
MS. SHAW: [7]*I'm very well,* thank you. And you?
MR. ABE: Fine, thanks. [8]*What kind of things* does your daughter like?
MS. SHAW: Well, she asked me to look for a Japanese fan.
MR. ABE: Well, we'll go to the Ginza area. There are a lot of good [9]*department stores* there.
MS. SHAW: [10]*That sounds fine.* Shall we go?

(*Later*)
MS. SHAW: Well, I'm sure my daughter will like this fan. It's beautiful.
MR. ABE: Good. Well, it's one o'clock. [11]*Would you like to have lunch* now?
MS. SHAW: Oh, yes, [12]*that's a great idea.* I'm pretty [13]*hungry now.*
MR. ABE: [14]*Do you like Japanese* food, or [15]*would you prefer* Western food?
MS. SHAW: Oh, I like Japanese food, especially soba.
MR. ABE: I know an excellent soba restaurant near here. Let's try that.

(*Later*)
MS. SHAW: That was delicious. [16]*Thank you very much* for helping me [17]*buy gifts.*
MR. ABE: [18]*That's all right.*

MS. SHAW: I [19]*really hate* shopping!
MR. ABE: So do I, but I [20]*enjoy shopping* for gifts.
MS. SHAW: Yes, I guess I do, too. But I [21]*prefer eating* in a nice restaurant after!

Activity 3

Conversation 1

A: My wife and I were wondering if you would like to come and spend the weekend with us at our home.
B: That's very kind of you. I'd like that very much.

Conversation 2

A: Hi, John! How about coming for a drink tonight after work?
B: Thanks. That sounds good.

Conversation 3

A: So, Ms. Smith. Would you like to visit the plant tomorrow?
B: Yes, Mr. White. Thank you very much. I'll look forward to that.

Conversation 4

A: Hello, Pat!
B: Hi, Tom!
A: Are you free this Friday?
B: Hmm, yes, I think so.
A: Well, we have an extra ticket for the concert on Friday. Why not join us?
B: Thanks, that's a great idea.

A – 4: invitation to a concert on Friday
B – 2: invitation to come for a drink after work
C – 1: invitation to spend the weekend at the couple's home
D – 3: invitation to visit the plant tomorrow

Invitation	1	2	3	4
Know each other well		✔		✔
Don't know each other well	✔		✔	

Activity 5

3: Thank you very much. I'll look forward to that.
4: Thanks. That's a great idea.
2: Thanks. That sounds good.
1: That's very kind of you. I'd like that very much.
Informal: 2 and 4

Activity 8

Conversation 1

A: If you have no plans for Sunday, would you like to join us for a picnic?
B: Thank you very much. That would be very nice.

Conversation 2

A: I was wondering if you would like to play golf on Saturday afternoon.
B: That's very kind of you, but I'm afraid I can't. I'm going to visit my grandparents this weekend.
A: Oh, what a pity! Perhaps another time.

Conversation 3

A: How about having lunch at the Italian restaurant?
B: Sorry, but I can't. I have to go to the dentist at lunchtime.
A: Oh, that's too bad!

Conversation 4

A: What about going to the club this evening?
B: Thanks, but I can't. I've got a date with my fiance.
A: Too bad. Maybe next time.
B: Yeah.

1 – ✔; 2 – X; 3 – X; 4 – X

That's very kind of you, but I'm afraid I can't. I'm going to visit my grandparents this weekend.
Sorry, but I can't. I have to go to the dentist at lunchtime.
Thanks, but I can't. I've got a date with my fiance.

Activity 10

Conversation 1

A: Would you like to go to dinner some time this week?
B: Yes, thank you very much. I'd love to.
A: Well, are you free on Thursday evening?
B: Yes, I am.
A: Good. I'll pick you up at your hotel at about 6:30.
B: That's fine. So I'll see you at the hotel on Thursday at 6:30. I'll be in the coffee shop.
A: Fine. See you Thursday, then. Goodbye.
B: Goodbye.

Conversation 2

A: Aah, Jean and I were wondering if you would like to come to our barbecue on Sunday afternoon?
B: That's very kind of you. That would be very nice.
A: Do you know how to get to our house?
B: Is it near the station?
A: Yes, it's very close. I can pick you up at the station if you like.
B: Oh, thank you. What time?
A: Is 2:30 OK?
B: Yes, that's fine.
A: Good. I'll see you at the station on Sunday at 2:30.

Conversation 3

A: Oh, hi, Helen! Um, I have an extra ticket for the new movie at the "Plaza" tomorrow evening. Would you like to come?
B: Sure! I'd love to come! What time should we meet?
A: Well, the movie starts at 7:30, so let's meet in front of the theater at 7:00.
B: That's fine. 7 o'clock in front of the "Plaza." See you then. Bye!
A: See you. Bye!

Invitation	To	Meeting Day/Time	Meeting Place
1	Dinner	Thursday/6:30	Hotel coffee shop
2	Barbecue	Sunday/2:30	Station
3	Movie	Tomorrow/7:00	In front of theater

Activity 11

Student responses in italics.

MR. BRAUN: Would you like to come to the beach with us on Saturday?
YOU: *Thank you very much. I'd love to come.*
MR. BRAUN: We'll meet just outside your hotel.
YOU: *About what time?*
MR. BRAUN: Is 10 a.m. all right?
YOU: *Yes, 10 a.m. is fine. So you'll meet me at 10 a.m. on Saturday just outside the hotel?*
MR. BRAUN: That's right. So we'll see you then. Goodbye.
YOU: *I'll look forward to it. Goodbye.*

Unit 4

Activity 1

1. T 2. F 3. F 4. T 5. T 6. F

Activity 2

MR. KASLAN: Have a seat, Mr. Bond.
MR. BOND: This is a nice restaurant.
MR. KASLAN: Yes, I often bring guests here. I like the food very much. Now, [1]*what would you like to eat?*
MR. BOND: Well, I've never eaten Indonesian food before. What [2]*would you recommend?*
MR. KASLAN: OK, let's look at the menu. [3]*Do you like* hot, spicy food?
MR. BOND: Well, yes, but I don't really like *very* spicy food.
MR. KASLAN: In that case, [4]*I'd recommend* some sate ayam. That's small pieces of chicken, grilled on a skewer. It comes with a special sauce.
MR. BOND: That sounds good.
MR. KASLAN: [5]*Do you like* seafood?
MR. BOND: Oh, yes, [6]*I like it very much.*
MR. KASLAN: Well, [7]*how about* some sambal goreng udang? That's shrimp fried in a coconut sauce. And we'll have some vegetables, too. Gado-gado should be nice.
MR. BOND: What's gado-gado?
MR. KASLAN: It's a mixed vegetable salad with a peanut sauce. And we'll have some plain boiled rice.
MR. BOND: [8]*That sounds fine.*
MR. KASLAN: [9]*Would you like anything* to drink?
MR. BOND: Yes, please. What goes best with sate ayam and udang?
MR. KASLAN: [10]*I'd recommend* Bintang beer. We don't usually drink anything stronger with our meals.
MR. BOND: Fine. Do you use chopsticks in Indonesia, Mr. Kaslan?
MR. KASLAN: Oh, no, we use a fork and a spoon. Well, let's order.

(Later)

MR. KASLAN: [11]*Please start,* Mr. Bond.

(Later)

MR. KASLAN: [12]*Would you like* some fruit?

MR. BOND: Well, I've had plenty to eat, but [13]*what do you suggest?*

MR. KASLAN: [14]*Why not try* some tropical fruit? Rambutan is very refreshing.

MR. BOND: Mmm, they look interesting. How do you eat them?

MR. KASLAN: Press them at the top. The skin will break, so you can remove it. Then just bite into it. But be careful — there's a big pit inside.

MR. BOND: [15]*Mmm, that was delicious.* They taste a bit like lychees.

MR. KASLAN: Would you like [16]*any more beer?*

MR. BOND: Oh, no, thank you, [17]*I've had plenty.* That was a delicious meal. Thank you very much. And [18]*thanks for explaining* all the dishes to me.

MR. KASLAN: My pleasure. I'm glad you enjoyed it. We'll have some real Javanese coffee in a coffee shop near here.

Activity 3

1. d 2. c 3. b 4. a

Accepted: 2 and 4 Declined: 1 and 3

Activity 7

Mr. Bond	**Mr. Kaslan**
What would you recommend?	*I'd recommend some sate ayam.*
What goes best with sate ayam and udang?	I'd recommend Bintang beer.
What do you suggest?	*Why not try some tropical fruit?*

Activity 8

1. coq au vin — red wine
2. curry — beer
3. caviar — vodka
4. sweet and sour fish — Chinese green tea
5. sashimi — sake

Activity 9

Suggested answers in italics:

MR. GOMEZ: So, Mr. Balendra, [1]*what would you like to eat?*

MR. BALENDRA: Oh, I don't really know much about Mexican food. [2]*What would you recommend?*

MR. GOMEZ: Well, [3]*do you like* spicy food?

MR. BALENDRA: Yes, [4]*I like it very much.*

MR. GOMEZ: Good. In that case, [5]*I'd recommend* guacamole and nachos to start with, followed by enchiladas and hot sauce.

MR. BALENDRA: That [6]*sounds good.*

MR. GOMEZ: [7]*Would you like anything to drink?*

MR. BALENDRA: What do you suggest?

MR. GOMEZ: [8]*How about some* tequila?

MR. BALENDRA: Fine. [9]*How do you eat* the guacamole?

MR. GOMEZ: Just dip the nachos into the guacamole and eat them with your fingers.

	(Later)
MR. GOMEZ:	Would you like anything more to eat or drink?
MR. BALENDRA:	No, thank you. [10]*I've had plenty.*
MR. GOMEZ:	Did you enjoy your first Mexican meal?
MR. BALENDRA:	[11]*Yes, very much, thank you. It was delicious.*
MR. GOMEZ:	My pleasure. I'm glad you liked it.

Activity 10

Suggested answer

"Well, in that case, I'd recommend the chicken/the meat," etc.

Mr. Kaslan would have recommended something on the menu without seafood.

Activity 11

Conversation 1

A: Well, Mr. Rix, do you like steak?
B: No.
A: Oh, I see. Ahmm . . . well, do you like fish?
B: Not much.
A: Ah . . .

Conversation 2

A: Well, Mr. Rix, what would you like to eat? How about some steak?
B: Well, I'd really prefer chicken or fish.
A: OK. In that case, I suggest the roast chicken. It's always very good here.
B: Mmm, yes, that sounds good.

Conversation 2 is better: In Conversation 1, the person does not express any other preferences, so it is difficult for the host to suggest other dishes on the menu.

Activity 13

1. b 2. c 3. a

Unit 5

Activity 1

1. T 2. F 3. T 4. F 5. F 6. F

Activity 2

MR. WANG:	[1]*Are you enjoying the conference* so far, Mr. Hakim?
MR. HAKIM:	Yes, I've learned some new things today. And [2]*where exactly are you from,* Mr. Wang?
MR. WANG:	[3]*I'm from Taipei* in Taiwan. [4]*I work for* Ace Computer Company in Taipei. It's a subsidiary of Ace Electronics in Japan.
MR. HAKIM:	I see, and [5]*what do you do?*
MR. WANG:	I'm a systems analyst. Most of the time, I'm in Taipei, but I usually go to Tokyo once a year to visit our head office.
MR. HAKIM:	[6]*Do you live in Taipei?*
MR. WANG:	No, I live just outside the city. It's much quieter. And what about you? [7]*What's your job?*
MR. HAKIM:	I 'm an engineer with the Malaysian Television Authority.
MR. WANG:	[8]*Where do you live?*

MR. HAKIM: In Kuala Lumpur, but I used to live in Kota Kinabalu.

MR. WANG: That's in Sabah, isn't it?

MR. HAKIM: That's right. I was transferred to Kuala Lumpur two years ago.

MR. WANG: [9]*Did you like Sabah?*

MR. HAKIM: Yes, I liked it very much. [10]*My job was very interesting.* But I'm afraid my wife didn't enjoy it at all! So she is very happy now in Kuala Lumpur.

MR. WANG: I visited Kuala Lumpur last year on a business trip. But I didn't see very much because I had only one day free, and it rained!

MR. HAKIM: Oh, that's too bad. Well, if you get the chance to visit again, my wife and I will be happy to show you around.

MR. WANG: [11]*That's very kind of you.* Thank you.

(Sound of bell)

MR. HAKIM: Well, [12]*the next session begins* in a few minutes. Which talk are you going to now, Mr. Wang?

MR. WANG: I 'd like to hear the talk by Dr. Ogawa. It's in room 20.

MR. HAKIM: I'm going to room 3. [13]*It was very nice meeting you,* Mr. Wang.

MR. WANG: Yes, [14]*it was nice meeting you, too.* I hope [15]*we'll see each other again.* Goodbye.

MR. HAKIM: [16]*Goodbye.*

Activity 3

Conversation 1

A: Well, I thought the last talk was very good. What did you think?

B: Yes, the presentation was very interesting. The speaker was well-prepared.

A: Where are you from, Mr. Lee?

B: I'm from Singapore, but I work here.

A: Oh, I see. What do you do?

B: I'm a research engineer with Brown Electronics. We have a plant here. What about you?

A: Well, . . .

Conversation 2

A: Well, I thought the last talk was very good. Did you?

B: Yes.

A: Hmm. Uh, are you from Seoul?

B: No.

A: Oh. Where are you from?

B: Singapore.

A: Ah . . . What do you do?

B: I'm a research engineer.

A: Aah . . .

a. The first conversation is better. The second speaker offers more information and does not just answer "Yes" or "No." He also asks questions. Also, in the first conversation, the first speaker starts with an "opinion" question: "*What did you think?*" This forces the second speaker to say more than just "Yes" or "No."

Activity 4

1. c 2. d 3. b 4. a

Activity 5

MR. DAVIES: So, Mr. Stein, are you enjoying the seminar?
MR. STEIN: Yes, very much. The last workshop was very interesting.
MR. DAVIES: Yes, it was. By the way, Mr. Stein, where are you from?
MR. STEIN: I'm from Switzerland.
MR. DAVIES: Oh, where exactly in Switzerland?
MR. STEIN: I'm from Basel. Do you know it?
MR. DAVIES: No, but I visited Zurich last year on business. Do you work in Basel, too?
MR. STEIN: No, I'm working in Bangkok now.
MR. DAVIES: I see, and what do you do?
MR. STEIN: I'm the Product Research Consultant for Meyer Drugs. Our Southeast Asia office is based in Bangkok. What about you? . . .

1. Are you enjoying the seminar?
2. Where are you from?
3. Where exactly in Switzerland?
4. Do you work in Basel, too?
5. What do you do?

Activity 7

PAUL: Hello, Mai! Well, are you enjoying the trade fair so far?
MAI: Hi there, Paul. Yes, it's really exciting.
PAUL: Oh, Mike, let me introduce you to Mai Manoon. She's from Thailand. Mai, this is Mike Drew.
MIKE: How do you do, Ms. Manoon? It's nice to meet you.
MAI: How do you do, Mr. Drew? Nice to meet you, too.
MIKE: Where are you from in Thailand, Ms. Manoon?
MAI: From Songhkla, but I'm working in Hong Kong now. I live on Lantau Island.
MIKE: Oh, I see. And what do you do there?
MAI: I work for Sarina Clothing. I'm the Overseas Sales Manager. What about you?
MIKE: Well, I'm also working overseas. I'm from Sydney, Australia, but I only go there twice a year. I'm based in Manila, in the Philippines. I work at the head office of Polar Soft Drinks. I'm the Advertising Director for Southeast Asia. How about you, Paul? Are you still with Trident?
PAUL: Yes. I got promoted to Executive Director last year.
MIKE: Congratulations! Are you still living in New York?
PAUL: No, I moved to the Washington office last year.
MAI: Do you live in Washington?
PAUL: No, I live in Arlington, Virginia. It's much nicer than Washington!
MAI & MIKE: I'm sure it is!

Name	Job	Company	Work-Place	Residence
Mai Manoon	*Overseas Sales Manager*	*Sarina Clothing*	*Hong Kong*	Lantau Island
Paul Slade	*Executive Director*	Trident Photocopiers	*Washington*	*Arlington, Virginia*
Mike Drew	Advertising Director	*Polar Soft Drinks*	*Manila*	*Manila Philippines*

Activity 9

Conversation 1

A: So, Mr. Black, what did you think of the last discussion?

B: Oh, the first speaker was very good. He made a lot of interesting points.

A: Yes, I agree. His presentation was excellent. But the other speaker was awful!

B: That's true. He tried to give too many details. . . .

Conversation 2

A: Excuse me, but I think we're staying at the same hotel. I think I saw you at breakfast.

B: Oh, yes, I remember. It's a very nice hotel, isn't it?

A: Yes, I'm very pleased with my room this year. Last year I had a *very* small room with no air-conditioning.

B: Oh, how awful. I think the management is new—the service is *much* better than last year. Would you like some coffee? . . .

Conversation 3

A: Do you know what time lunch is?

B: I think it's from 12:30 to 1:30, but I'm not sure. . . .

C: I have the schedule here, let me check. . . . Yes, you're right, 12:30 to 1:30.

A: Oh, good. I'll be ready for lunch! That was a long morning.

B: It certainly was!

Conversation 4

A: Have you been to Bangkok before, Mr. Suzuki?

B: Yes, I was here ten years ago for my honeymoon. I suppose the city has changed a lot since then.

A: Well, if you take the tour of the city tomorrow, you will find out.

B: Yes, I'd like that. But perhaps it's too late to get a reservation?

A: I don't think so. Let's check with the tour organizer. . . .

Conversation	1	2	3	4
Topic	*Speakers/ Presentations*	*Hotel Accom-modation*	*Lunch Arrange-ments*	*Conference Location/ Sightseeing*

Ending a Conversation

Mr. Hakim's signal was, "Well, the next session begins in a few minutes . . ."

Activity 11

Conversation 1

A: Well, I must go.
B: Oh, well . . .
A: Bye!

Conversation 2

A: Well, it's rather late. Perhaps we should leave. It was very nice talking to you.
B: Yes, it was nice talking to you, too. I hope we'll meet again some time.
A: Yes, so do I. Goodbye.
B: Goodbye.

1. The second conversation is better. The first speaker gives a clearer signal to the other person.
   In the first conversation, the first speaker is very abrupt, and does not allow the second speaker to finish the conversation. The first speaker seems impolite.
2. "It's rather late. Perhaps we should leave."

Activity 12

Conversation 1

A: Well, I'm afraid I have to go now. I'm having dinner with my boss in an hour.
B: I see. Well, it was nice talking to you. See you next week.

Conversation 2

A: Oh, is it 5 o'clock already? I'm sorry, but I'll have to leave you now. I have to be at the airport at 6:30. My plane leaves at 7:30.
B: Well, it was nice meeting you. Perhaps we'll see each other at next year's conference.

Conversation 3

A: I'd like to talk longer, but I really have to go now. I have to finish my report for tomorrow's presentation.
B: I understand. I'll see you there tomorrow.

1: 1. c 2. a 3. b
2: 1: *I'm afraid I have to go now.*
2: *Is it 5 o'clock already?* I'm sorry, but *I'll have to leave you now.*
3: *I'd like to talk longer,* but *I really have to go now.*

Unit 6

Activity 1

1. F 2. F 3. F 4. T 5. F 6. T

Activity 2

MR. SATO: That was a delicious meal, Mr. Barr. Thank you very much.
MR. BARR: My pleasure. Do you have any plans for this afternoon?
MR. SATO: No, not really.
MR. BARR: Well, in that case, [1]*would you like me to show you around* the town? St. Andrews is quite an interesting place.
MR. SATO: [2]*Yes, that's very kind of you.* I'd love to do some sightseeing.
MR. BARR: Well, if you're ready, let's go.

That building in front of us is the Royal and Ancient Golf Club, but you probably know that already?
MR. SATO: Yes, it's quite well-known in Japan. [3]*Would it be possible to look inside* some time?
MR. BARR: Yes, [4]*that's no problem.* I'm a club member. I'll take you there tomorrow if you like. We'll go along this street. Now on the right is one of the older parts of the university. Let's go in this way. This is called the "Quad."
MR. SATO: [5]*This is lovely.* How old is the university?
MR. BARR: Well, it was founded in 1412 AD, so it's over 500 years old.
MR. SATO: How interesting. [6]*What's that building* over there?
MR. BARR: That's the university chapel, a church for the students.
MR. SATO: [7]*Is it all right if* I take photographs inside?
MR. BARR: [8]*Yes, it is.*
Now let's go out this way and we'll go to the cathedral.

MR. SATO: Is [9]*the cathedral still used*?
MR. BARR: No, I'm afraid it's mostly in ruins now.
MR. SATO: [10]*It's really beautiful,* isn't it? What's that tower?
MR. BARR: St. Rule's Tower. You get a wonderful view from the roof.
MR. SATO: [11]*Can we go up to the roof*?
MR. BARR: I'm [12]*afraid not.* Visitors aren't allowed to go up because the stairs are broken. It's too dangerous.
MR. SATO: What a pity.
MR. BARR: I'll take you down to the castle now.
MR. SATO: [13]*When was it* built?
MR. BARR: I'm not sure, but I think it's older than the university.

(*Later*)
Well, Mr. Sato, are you tired? [14]*Would you like to have a rest?*
MR. SATO: Well, yes, I am beginning to feel a bit tired.
MR. BARR: Would [15]*you like me to drive you back to your hotel?*
MR. SATO: Oh, thank you, but [16]*please don't bother.* It's not far.
[17]*What an interesting* tour. Thank you.
MR. BARR: I'm glad [18]*you enjoyed it.* I'll call you tomorrow. Goodbye.
MR. SATO: Fine. Goodbye and [19]*thanks again.*

Activity 3 1. b 2. c 3. a

Activity 4

1. I have an extra ticket for the golf tournament this weekend. *Would you like it?*
2. If you're going shopping, *would you like to borrow my car for the afternoon*? I won't be going out.
3. *Should I arrange a meeting tomorrow with the branch representatives?*

Activity 7

Conversation 1

ROOM SERVICE: Hello, Room Service. Can I help you?
MR. SATO: Hello. This is room 407. Could I have a pot of coffee and some sandwiches, please?
RS: Certainly, sir. What kind of sandwiches?
MR. SATO: Oh, um, chicken, please.
RS: Right, sir. That's room 407, is that correct?
MR. SATO: Yes, that's right.
RS: They'll be up in about 15 minutes, sir.
MR. SATO: Thank you.

Conversation 2

MR. SATO: Well, Mr. Jones, thank you very much for the tour of your research laboratory. It was very interesting.
MR. JONES: I'm glad you enjoyed it. Where would you like to go now?
MR. SATO: Well, I'd like to go back to my hotel. Could you arrange a taxi for me, please?
MR. JONES: Yes, that's no problem. I'll just get the receptionist to call for one.

Conversation 3

TRAVEL AGENT: Good afternoon. Can I help you?
MR. SATO: Good afternoon. Yes, could you confirm my return flight to Osaka, please? Here's my ticket.
TRAVEL AGENT: Of course, sir. Please take a seat.

Conversation 4

RECEPTIONIST: Good morning, Mr. Sato. What can I do for you? I hope your room is all right?
MR. SATO: Good morning. Yes, it's fine, thank you. Would it be possible to send a fax to Japan?
RECEPTIONIST: I'm sorry, but the hotel fax machine is out of order. You could try the bookstore across the street. They have one.
MR. SATO: Oh, thank you very much.

1. Hotel 2. Research laboratory 3. Travel agent's 4. Hotel reception

1. *Certainly, sir.*
2. *Could you arrange* a taxi for me, please?
   Yes, that's no problem.
3. *Could you confirm* my return flight to Osaka, please?
   Of course, sir.
4. *Would it be possible* to send a fax to Japan?
   I'm sorry, but the hotel fax machine is out of order.

Activity 8 1. c 2. a 3. b

Activity 9

MRS. BARR: Hello again, Mr. Sato. It's nice to see you again. Please come in. John's in the living room. Just go straight ahead.
MR. SATO: Hello, Mrs. Barr. It's nice to see you again, too. I've brought you some flowers.
MRS. BARR: Oh, you shouldn't have, but they are lovely! Thank you.
MR. SATO: Oh, what a beautiful white carpet! Uh . . . is it all right if I take off my shoes?
MRS. BARR: Take off your shoes? Well . . . we don't usually, but if you would feel more comfortable, please go ahead.
MR. SATO: Oh, no, no, it's all right. I'll keep them on.
MR. BARR: Now then, Mr. Sato, what would you like to drink? Whisky, gin, some wine?
MR. SATO: Some wine would be nice, thank you.
MRS. BARR: So, Mr. Sato, what do you think of St. Andrews . . . ?

MRS. BARR: Well, would you all like to come through to the dining room? Now, you sit here next to me, Mr. Sato. I hope you like salmon. Please help yourself to vegetables.
MR. SATO: That was delicious, Mrs. Barr. I love salmon.
MRS. BARR: I'm glad you enjoyed it.
MR. BARR: Would you like some cheese and crackers with your coffee?
MR. SATO: Oh, I've had plenty to eat. Just coffee, thank you. Uh, . . . would you mind if I smoke?
MR. BARR: Well, I'm afraid I'm allergic to cigarette smoke.
MR. SATO: Oh, I see. Is it all right if I go outside to the garden to smoke?
MR. BARR: Yes, certainly. I'll show you round.

MR. SATO: You have such a lovely house and garden. May I take a photograph of you and Mrs. Barr out in the garden?
MR. BARR: Of course. Meg! Come on out here. Mr. Sato wants to take a picture!

MR. SATO: Well, thank you for a wonderful meal, Mrs. Barr.
MRS. BARR: I'm glad you could come.
MR. SATO: Can I use your phone to call a taxi?
MR. BARR: Yes, but that won't be necessary. I'll drive you back to your hotel.
MR. SATO: Oh, that's very kind of you.
MR. BARR: Not at all. Well, if you're ready . . . ?

1. take off his shoes (yes); smoke (no); go into the garden to smoke (yes); take a photograph of Mr. and Mrs. Barr (yes); use the phone (yes, but not necessary)
2. Is it all right if I take off my shoes?
   Would you mind if I smoke?
   Is it all right if I go outside to the garden to smoke?
   May I take a photograph of you and Mrs. Barr out in the garden?
   Can I use your phone to call a taxi?

Activity 10 1. c 2. a 3. b

Activity 11

4 – Could I have an extra pillow, please?
1 – Can I help you with the dishes?
3 – Would you mind if I took a shower now?
2 – Do you mind if I watch the news on TV?

Activity 12

He is Japanese and it is the custom in Japan to take off your shoes in people's homes.

1 – Not usual in some parts of Asia/Southeast Asia/Middle East
2 – Not usual anywhere
3 – Usual everywhere
4 – Not usual except in Europe/North America in hot seasons
5 – Not usual in North America, Northern Europe
6 – Usual in Middle-East, parts of Southeast Asia/Asia
7 – Not usual in Europe/North America except for "dry" foods like sandwiches
8 – Not usual in North America, Europe
9 – Not usual in many parts of the Middle East